DEEP GLIMPSES

APPLIANCE GIFTS

Putting Spiritual Gifts into Service

P.J. ALLAN

Scripture taken from the New King James Version®. Copyright © 1982 by Thomas Nelson. Used by permission. All rights reserved.

Note: Bold and underlining in Scripture references added as emphasis and not indicative of original text.

Published by Deep Glimpses
www.deepglimpses.com
Print ISBN: 979-8-9928260-2-9
Ebook ISBN: 979-8-9928260-3-6

Printed in the United States

CONTENTS

THE GIFTS: NOT FOR SELF-ADORNMENT

T he first year my wife and I were married, we didn't have much of anything. We rented a small upstairs apartment in a rough area for eighty-five dollars a month. We didn't even have a driveway, so we had to park our cars on the street. Our first Christmas, I decided to get her a new vacuum cleaner ... because we didn't have one. On Christmas Day, she was delighted and appreciated the gift, but let's just say I could tell that it wasn't a homerun in the ideal gift selection. Though she never complained, I knew I needed to step up my game.

My wife loves to cook and is good at it, so the next Christmas, I gave her a food processor. Okay, okay, I know once again, I probably could have done better, but she loved it and used it all the time. I know it's not really a personal item. It's not a gold chain or freshwater pearl earrings. And fortunately, she never demanded these types of things. But how desperate would she have to be to take her vacuum cleaner and food processor, hang them on a chain, and go out wearing them around her neck showing off her appliances? I know, it sounds ridiculous, right?

Then why is it that some believers in Christ seem to do the exact same thing when it comes to the gifts of the Spirit? It appears they adorn themselves with their received gifts to the point of wearing these gifts like they were medals of honor or awards giving them VIP access to the show. It was during our early years of marriage and these times of struggle that I realized the gifts of the Spirit were also *service* or *appliance* gifts.

As we continue through our study together, I'm hoping we can all grasp the access we have to these gifts and how they should be used for cleaning, building, healing, correcting, and strengthening the house of the Lord—not for self-adornment.

(Looking good!)

JESUS IS LORD: EMBRACING THE US-NESS OF THE KINGDOM

Let's begin by looking at 1 Corinthians chapter 12.

> *Now concerning spiritual gifts, brethren, I do not want you to be ignorant: You know that you were Gentiles, carried away to these dumb idols, however you were led. Therefore I make known to you that no one speaking by the Spirit of God calls Jesus accursed, and no one can say that Jesus is Lord except by the Holy Spirit.*
>
> *—1 Corinthians 12:1–3*

As we approach the gifts of the Holy Spirit, there is first a filter gate that we must pass through . . . and that gate is 'Jesus Is Lord'! This confession or awareness is essential for the Holy Spirit to gain access to our hearts. The first words we speak in the Holy Spirit are Jesus is Lord, and the first gift we receive is grace. There is a beautiful exchange within the Father, Son, and Holy Spirit, in that they work together in tandem. Each one glorifies the other. I know many struggle with the idea of the Trinity and find it difficult to understand. The way I see this is that if the center of God was an "I," God would be an egocentric, self-absorbed narcissist. But in view of the Trinity, the center of God's heart is an "US." Jesus prayed that we might be one with them as they are one.

> *Now I am no longer in the world, but these are in the world, and I come to You. Holy Father, keep through Your name those whom You have given Me, that they may be one as We are.*
>
> —*John 17:11*

> *I do not pray for these alone, but also for those who will believe in Me through their word; that they all may be one, as You, Father, are in Me, and I in You; that they also may be one in <u>Us</u>, that the world may believe that You sent Me.*
>
> —*John 17:20–21*

I believe a key component to operating in the gifts of the Spirit is first to embrace the "us-ness" of the kingdom. If you look at the Lord's prayer in Matthew 6, the whole prayer is in the plural.

> *In this manner, therefore, pray:*
> <u>*Our*</u> *Father in heaven,*
> *Hallowed be your name.*

Your kingdom come,
Your will be done,
On earth as it is in heaven.
Give us this day our daily bread,
And forgive us our debts,
As we forgive our debtors.
And do not lead us into temptation,
But deliver us from the evil one.
For Yours is the kingdom and the power and the glory
forever. Amen.

—Matthew 6:9–13[*]

Accepting Jesus is accepting the us-ness of God. This "I" thing has to go. I really believe that this is key. It's not about you—it's about us. At age two, we learn the word "mine" and spend the rest of our lives trying to get over it. Accepting Christ is accepting the oneness in the Father, Son, and Holy Spirit, as well as accepting that we are in this grace together. The continuation of this partnership in the Trinity is seen in the next few verses.

Now there are diversities of gifts, but the same Spirit.
There are differences of ministries, but the same Lord.
And there are diversities of activities, but it is the same
God who works in all.

—1 Corinthians 12:4–6

---

[*] *emphasis added*

I think most people read this quickly and assume that Paul is just writing the same thing in three different ways. But that's not the case. Paul is showing here the operation of the Trinity in action as it relates to how the gifts of the Spirit work to their full and accurate manifestation.

Gifts = Spirit   Ministries = Lord   Activities = God

The first thing is to notice the word "diversities"—diversities of gifts, differences of ministries, and diversities of activities. This opens up a realm of possibilities that is difficult to box in or set strict limits on, which I think better facilitates a confident dependency on the Holy Spirit to have control. If fact, there are different gifts mentioned in other parts of Scripture that go beyond the gifts mentioned here. Hopefully, we'll get to include these later.

Remember that "Jesus is Lord" is the key and is sustained in this realm of Holy Spirit manifestation and operation. To say "Jesus is Lord" declares He is either Lord of everything—or He's not Lord at all. You can have a gift without a ministry, and you can have a ministry without effect. Let's look at how these three distinct ways the gifts, services, and activities work together. The first part is found in verse 4.

Now there are diversities of gifts, but the same Spirit.[*]

We need to understand that the gifts are distributed by and in the control of the Holy Spirit. And that it is the same Spirit

---

[*] *emphasis added*

behind each diverse expression of the various gifts. In other words, whatever the expression of the gift, they all have the same Spirit in them working through them. I don't believe we can lay claim to these gifts as though they are ours. For when we do, we take control of that gift, and that's why there can be a different spirit at work. I've seen people try to implement a "gift" in anger, pride, control, and even lust. That is not the same Spirit we must keep in control of the gifts. We may have been used often by the Holy Spirit in a specific gift, but it still does not make that *our* gift. And why would anyone want to be restricted to one specific gift and limit how the Spirit may choose to use them? That's why the next verse is so important to understand. Let's take a look at verse 5.

There are differences of ministries, but the same Lord.

Okay, this is not talking about gifts any longer, but rather pointing to *how these gifts are to be used in ministries.* Other versions use "service" in place of ministries, but it's the same point. I believe this is meant to allow the gifts given to us to be submitted in service back to the lordship of Jesus Christ. Remember, Jesus is Lord! If you have a gift without a sanctioned venue or channel for that gift to function in the body, that gift is stifled. It has potential, but won't have effect without the Lord giving you instruction as to how that gift is to be used. His blessing and partnership keep the gift and the purpose on the same track.

Now let's take a look at verse 6.

> *There are diversities of activities, but it is the same*
> *God who works in all.*

Here we have the final blessing of the triune God working in complete harmony. Again, this is not about gifts, but activities or work. This has to do with the actual effect, the change that occurs as a result of a gift being applied in a ministry and its ultimate outcome or manifestation. The work is now the completed work. Something has changed; the gift applied has made a difference.

For example, with a gift of healing, you would be led by the Lord to pray for a specific person at a specific time, and the result or work is that the person is healed. Can you see now why it's so important to keep the gifts in the hands of the Holy Spirit, Jesus, and the Father? We can also see what happens when this union is out of sync. You could have a gift, but it's not been submitted to the Lord's direction. You use the gift in a self-directed way.

As another example, consider a rifle, which has power, process, and effect. The three main components are a bullet, a rifle, and a target. Let's say the bullet is the gift, the rifle is the ministry or service, and the target is the actual activity or accomplishment. So someone may say that they have a gift. That's like saying you have a bullet. And by itself, a bullet has no power. People without a Lord-given ministry or service application for that gift are like people throwing bullets at you. They have this gift, and they are going to use it. Only it's not having much effect. Now, someone who has a gift *and* a ministry loads the rifle and just starts shooting—still no effect, just a lot of smoke and noise. Now let's put them all together. You have a gift from the Holy Spirit, and you prayerfully submit to the Lord and ask how He would have you use this gift. The Lord directs you to a specific person, so you wait for the right time. Finally, you get the green light to put the gift into service, and the person is changed by the interaction. You put the bullet in the rifle and hit the target. The outcome is a clear manifestation of Jesus as Lord. This same summary is stated at the last part of verse 6.

But it is the same God who works in all.

When this continuity is intact and the three aspects all work together, the Lord gets the glory. We are building His house and these manifestations are humbly done as our service for His glory.

AN APPLIANCE GIFT
IMPROVES THE HOUSE

I f you live with a family, you understand that the chores required are for the benefit of everyone. Then you also understand that this struggle gets real, especially with the kids. The selfish entitlement of "I don't want to" or the declaration of "I did the dishes" when the job is done is heard in echoes of expecting accolades or reward. The next verse only accentuates that these manifestations are given to care for the whole house.

> But the manifestation of the Spirit is given to <u>each one</u>
> for the <u>profit of all</u>.*

Here is the "us" thing again in verse 7. I don't want to keep beating this drum, but if we can get this perspective right, it will change everything. The "us" of the Godhead is the Spirit who must be in charge of this realm of spiritual gifts and their manifestations in order for the church to rise to its destined glory.

---

* *emphasis added*

Going back to the "varieties" mentioned earlier, let me ask you how many varieties of tools, appliances, and cleaning products you have in order to maintain your home—lawn mowers, leaf blowers, snow shovels, vacuum cleaners, brooms, mops, pots, pans, etc. Each has a unique purpose and is mostly used without much fanfare. It's just what they do. Building the "us" in the family instead of facilitating an environment of various "I's" coexisting will determine the strength and longevity of the family unit. This is at the very heart of the Godhead and is why their kingdom will never end—and we are privileged to be included in that number by His grace.

Please note that the beginning of this verse uses the phrase "to each." The inference here is that everyone has something to contribute in this process. I am not sure how to facilitate this variety of giftings other than to say that it is impossible to include them in our current structure of church. Now, the traditional church service can facilitate many gifts, but it is limited by time and purpose thereby excluding many other giftings.

Pardon me while I dream a little, but what if instead of trying to fit the body of Christ into a limited environment and system, we allowed the manifestation of His Spirit and gifts to define our form? You know, *form follows function*. Now, I'm not suggesting one over the other, but rather that we recognize the true body of Christ is called to operate everywhere His people are and more than just once or twice a week. It is unfair to assume that all we need is the church meeting. In fact, if we buy into that limitation to our spiritual life, we are actually forging a duplicity in our lives and could end up double-minded.

Legitimate operations of the spiritual gifts will not and cannot always be sanctioned, limited, or timed. I believe if we begin to do this right, we may not even notice when these gifts manifest. Back to the home comparison. Once we're used to doing things around the house, we'll pick up something off the floor, throw it away, and not even think about it. No longer looking for or needing accolades and acknowledgement. When we are born again, we inherited a new nature. The more we grow in that nature, the more natural we become. In other words, the more spiritual I become, the more a spiritual things come naturally. Now, I'm not saying that we should take this realm lightly or casually. But when we are walking in the Spirit, this type of thing can happen automatically without a need for validation or sanction. Consider the words of Jesus in Matthew:

> *But when you do a charitable deed, do not let your left*
> *hand know what your right hand is doing, that your*
> *charitable deed may be in secret; and your Father who*
> *sees in secret will Himself reward you openly.*
>
> —*Matthew 6:3–4*

I know this text primarily applies to giving aid or charity, but I don't believe this attitude is limited and can definitely encompass spiritual gifts. You may recall when Jesus was being pressed by the crowd that a woman touched the hem of His garment and was healed. It happened naturally although Jesus did notice the touch and confirmed her healing.

PERSONAL ASSESSMENT: WHERE DO YOU DRAW THE LINE?

Do not give what is holy to the dogs; nor cast your pearls before swine, lest they trample them under their feet, and turn and tear you in pieces.

—Matthew 7:6

When I first read this seemingly obscure verse, I had no idea the tremendous influence and insights it would bring into the practical application of a balanced life. When I say *balanced life*, I mean the balance that comes from what God has given to you *for you* and what God has given to you *for the sole purpose of giving it away.* Oftentimes, things like wisdom, skills, and talents are really meant to be used for employment opportunities or community service.

Do not give what is holy to the dogs; nor cast your pearls before swine.

Here we see a clear distinction of two categories—dogs and pigs, holy and pearls. Let's look at the first pair. In the times of this teaching, Christ was using dogs and pigs in the sense of their ravenous appetites. Both will eat everything put before them to the point of getting sick. They don't know their level of intake and don't know when to say enough. The other pair mentioned are *holy* and *pearls.* This is meant to be set apart, separate, and hid away from those consumers who would take everything and squander it leaving you desolate or destroyed. This understanding is vital to anyone who would endeavor to operate in the realm of spiritual gifts.

Let's first look at what isn't said here. Jesus didn't say, "Don't give dogs dog food or pigs pig food." There is a portion of what we possess meant for others' benefit. Now, we're not calling those who receive our gifts dogs or pigs, but there can be times when the needs are desperate and can take much more than we are giving. Jesus also didn't say, "Don't share your pearls with pearl admirers or that which is holy with the holy." There are those who, when you share your pearls, put out a silk pillow to rest your pearls on and return them polished. And those who are holy know when what is being shared is of God and should be reverenced and respected. But if you share those same things with others who do not know how to handle them, they throw them around or disregard their value. They have no awareness of their worth and use your precious gift as a party favor, plaything, or toy.

Let me illustrate here what I'm trying to say.

The circle below represents everything in your life—your wealth, gifts, talents, possessions, skills, everything. The inner circle represents everything God has given to you for you. The outer part of the circle represents everything God has given you to share or give away. The inner circle is your *prosperity*, while the outer circle is your *charity*. Think about this for a minute. What things do you possess that benefit others?

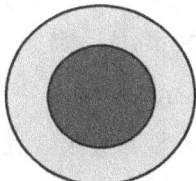

Remember that spiritual gifts are given for the profit of all, so they would be in the outer circle.

Some live their lives mostly for themselves and believe that everything God has given them is for them. There is not much room for spiritual gifts or charity.

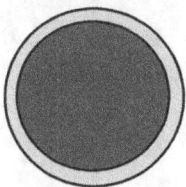

Others live completely open and have no boundaries. They believe they are to have nothing for themselves, and everything is out there for anybody and everybody. They will give away even vital essentials for their own well-being.

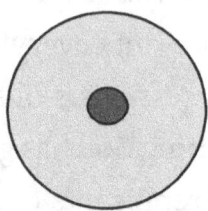

Let me give you a couple things to consider here.

1. It is completely between you and God to determine where that line is drawn.
2. People can use spiritual gifts selfishly as if they're for them and not the body.
3. Some give away too much and quickly burn out or get bitter, envious, and abusive.
4. You need to take an inventory of everything in your life before God and determine what God has given you to give back to Him or offer to others.

In the circles below draw an inner circle where you think you are now and in the second circle draw where you think you should be.

Where would you place Paul's line after reading 1 Corinthians 10:31–33?

> *Therefore, whether you eat or drink, or whatever you do, do all to the glory of God. Give no offense, either to the Jews or to the Greeks or to the church of God, just as I also please all men in all things, <u>not seeking my own profit, but the profit of many</u>, that they may be saved.*

Obviously, Paul was completely open to having everything he had being used for the Lord and those he was called to serve. I do believe some are called to this level of service and trust. We may aspire to live our lives this way and continue in our growth to where we too could say, "For to me, to live is Christ, and to die is gain" (Philippians 1:21).

Overflow

There is another thing we must consider here. What is it that makes some people act like dogs or pigs from the above scripture reference? I believe it happens when someone's inner circle is allowed to grow beyond the outer circle. Everything that God has given them is not enough, so now they want what God has given to others.

This is where people feel entitled and are envious toward others and their possessions. The sad truth is that once you go beyond what God has given you, you will never know contentment or satisfaction. Unfortunately, we have a culture that has built society upon this ravenous appetite for acquiring more than we need. Some call it ambition, but there is a difference between being productive and fruitful with the gifts that God has given to you and striving to keep up with others productivity.

Fruitful production and growth starts with accepting the limited seed in your hand and doing something with it. In Luke 16:10 we read; "He who is faithful in what is least is faithful also in much; and he who is unjust in what is least is unjust also in much." But when this drive exceeds honest operations, it begins to hinder others from being productive by undermining their efforts and losing sight of correct priorities and values. This is why so many public agencies have long abandoned "customer care" and have made their priority profits over people.

This will eventually consume its carrier. Things like "Lust of the Flesh, Lust of the Eye and the Pride of Life," once enraged, will gradually consume the person who allowed its dominance in the first place. These can become miserable people who have no limit of intake and end up wasting all they have acquired. Their appetites turned them into ravenous individuals, who the Bible compares to dogs and swine.

GIFTS OPERATING BY GRACE

Having then <u>gifts</u> differing according to the <u>grace that is given to us</u>, let us use them: if prophecy, let us prophesy in proportion to our faith; or ministry, let us use it in our ministering; he who teaches, in teaching; he who exhorts, in exhortation; he who gives, with liberality; he who leads, with diligence; he who shows mercy, with cheerfulness.

—Romans 12:6–8*

Not only does Paul here include other gifts beyond those mentioned in 1 Corinthians 12, but he gives us insight into how these gifts are deposited and differ.

Gifts differing according to the grace that is given to us.

If we look into the Greek definitions, it actually becomes clearer that gifts are an extension or expanse of saving grace.

---

* *emphasis added*

The word for grace is *charis,* meaning "the divine influence upon the heart and its reflection in the life, gratitude, acceptable benefit, favor, gift, grace, joy, liberality, pleasure, thankworthy." The word for gift is *charisma,* meaning "gratuity, deliverance from danger or passion, a spiritual endowment, qualification, miraculous faculty, free gift."

Grace = Charis   *Gift = Charisma*

So if we have received the grace of God in our hearts, we can boldly declare JESUS IS LORD. In the same way, grace opens to extend gifts through and by grace. From CHARIS to CHARISMA. Peter opens this up further in 1 Peter 4:10–11.

> As <u>each</u> has received a <u>gift,</u> use it <u>to serve</u> <u>one another,</u> as <u>good stewards</u> of God's <u>varied grace:</u> whoever speaks, as one who speaks oracles of God; whoever serves, as one who serves by the strength that God supplies—in order that in everything God may be glorified through Jesus Christ. To him belong glory and dominion forever and ever. Amen.*

Here is a confirmation: We are stewards who serve the varied grace expressions of gifts to one another. Jesus is Lord!

One trap I see many fall into is using the gifts of the Spirit as a noun describing their ministries. "I am a Healer" or "I am a Prophet." In my experience, once someone identifies in such a manner, they seem to lose the actual power of that

---

* *emphasis added*

operational gift. My encouragement is to keep these gifts in the verb form. Allow them to stay in the hand of the Lord and keep them as action words and not a perch to begin a personal ministry platform.

THE KEY: The Third Component "Eucharis"

We just looked at how *charis* = grace and *charisma* = gifts, and we will now look at this word <u>eucharis</u>.

The Greek word *eucharis* is derived from the combination of *eu*, meaning "good" or "well," and *charis*, meaning "grace," "kindness," or "favor." Therefore, *eucharis* can be translated as "full of grace," "charming," or "grateful." It conveys a sense of beauty, favor, or thankfulness.

In different contexts, "eucharis" might also relate to concepts of gratitude or pleasing qualities. It is worth noting that the term is closely related to "eucharist," which in Christian theology refers to the sacrament of Holy Communion, stemming from the idea of giving thanks (from the Greek "eucharisteo," meaning "to give thanks").

Many miss this third most important part. Once someone has grace or favor in their heart toward another, they manifest that favor by an expression of that affection in a gift. Once that gift is received, there must be a reciprocal grace expressed in thanksgiving.

This act is actually giving the gift of grace back to the person who gave it initially.

Now it happened as He went to Jerusalem that He passed through the midst of Samaria and Galilee. Then as He entered a certain village, there met Him ten men who were lepers, who stood afar off. And they lifted up their voices and said, "Jesus, Master, have mercy on us!" So when He saw them, He said to them, "Go, show yourselves to the priests." And so it was that as they went, they were cleansed. And one of them, when he saw that he was healed, returned, and with a loud voice glorified God, and fell down on his face at His feet, giving Him thanks. And he was a Samaritan. So Jesus answered and said, "Were there not ten cleansed? But where are the nine? Were there not any found who returned to give glory to God except this foreigner?" And He said to him, "Arise, go your way. Your faith has made you well."

—Luke 17:11–19

There has been speculation whether the other nine sustained their healing. Here lies the difference between receiving a gift and taking a gift. Those who never follow through with returning the gift in thanksgiving, acknowledging that it was given by someone else to you. Thereby keeping the exchange intact. Charis, Charisma & Eucharis.

Abraham's Example

Many know the story of Abraham being the father of our faith. He heard the Lord and obeyed him and it was accounted unto him as righteousness. He was given a promise that he would be the father of a great nation, only he didn't have an heir. He tried to fulfill the promise in his own strength, as many recipients of grace also attempt to do. Finally, the promise was fulfilled through Sarah bearing Isaac. So far we can see "Charis" in the promise and "Charisma" in Isaac. But what about the third essential component? God called Abraham to offer his son Isaac as a sacrifice on an altar. To give God's gift back to God. Once that trifecta has been completed, the blessing of God begin to flow. Can you see why so many miss this vitally important part of the gifts? They never give them back to God to control or distribute. If the Gifts are in fact the Gifts of the Spirit, we best surrender them back in thanksgiving so that the Holy Spirit, the Lord Jesus Christ and our Heavenly Father can use us in the manifestation of His Gifts... Jesus is Lord!

This combination of *charis, charisma,* and *eucharis* is also seen throughout Israel's history in their celebration of the feasts. God would bless their harvest by giving them a good crop and Israel would bring "the first fruits" offering and give it back to the Lord. The concept of first fruits applied to the first of everything- crops, livestock, and even the firstborn of the people. The offering of first fruits symbolized giving God the first and best, trusting Him for the rest. In the New

Testament, this concept extended metaphorically to refer to Christ as the "first fruits" of the resurrection.

> *But now Christ is risen from the dead, and has be-*
> *come the firstfruits of those who have fallen asleep.*
> *For since by man came death, by Man also came the*
> *resurrection of the dead. For as in Adam all die, even*
> *so in Christ all shall be made alive. But each one in his*
> *own order: Christ the firstfruits, afterward those who*
> *are Christ's at His coming.*

> *—1 Corinthians 15:20–23*

God's grace toward man gave us the gift of His Son sacrificed for our sins. The resurrection of Christ is the result of His victory and the start of Christ's return to His Father, which actually happened on the Feast of First Fruits, giving back the gift. And that released the power of the Holy Spirit, also on the Feast of Pentecost, to empower and multiply the Body of Christ throughout time and the whole earth.

And James refers to born-again believers as the first fruits of Salvation.

> *Of His own will He brought us forth by the word of*
> *truth, that we might be a kind of firstfruits of His*
> *creatures.*

> *—James 1:18*

So once we realize that by Gods grace we have been given a gift, we are then to return that gift as an offering of praise and thanksgiving to God. I believe this puts these powerful manifestations of heaven back into the only hands that can wield them accurately.

Back to the Gifts

For to one is given the word of wisdom through the Spirit, to another the word of knowledge through the same Spirit, to another faith by the same Spirit, to another gifts of healings by the same Spirit, to another the working of miracles, to another prophecy, to another discerning of spirits, to another different kinds of tongues, to another the interpretation of tongues. But one and the same Spirit works all these things, distributing to each one individually as He <u>wills</u>.

—1 Corinthians 12:8–11[*]

I am not going to develop each of these gifts extensively because I believe that, for the most part, they are self-explanatory. I will make a few distinctions, but more important is that we get the premise of the "us" purpose as well as the possibility that these gifts can operate almost unnoticed.

---

[*] *emphasis added*

For to one is given the word of wisdom through the Spirit, to another the word of knowledge through the same Spirit.

These two gifts can be expressed in conversation, in counseling, or in a sermon. Wisdom and knowledge, when expressed through a gift of the Spirit, come across AMPED. There is a natural wisdom and knowledge, and then there is a supernatural impartation when speaking under the influence of the Holy Spirit. From my experience, when this happens, I don't stop the conversation and highlight, "Hey, that was a word of wisdom there, you know, just in case you missed it." If, in fact, it was a word spoken by the Holy Spirit, the person hearing it was fully aware that it was the Lord speaking to them.

To another faith by the same Spirit, to another gifts of healings by the same Spirit.

Faith, by its very nature, in and of itself, is unseen. Jesus once said that if you have faith the size of a mustard seed, you can move mountains. You don't see the mustard seed faith, just the manifestation of faith in action. James said that he will show his faith by his works. The writer of Hebrews defines faith in this way:

Now faith is the substance of things hoped for, the evidence of things not seen.

—Hebrews 11:1

Faith is a substance and an evidence of things not seen. We all have faith of some sort in something. When the gift of faith is imparted by the Holy Spirit, there is a surge of strength in believing. What may have been previously hard to believe is now a certain absolute.

*To another gifts (plural) of healings by the same Spirit.**

Once again, there is a natural healing. If we cut our finger, it can naturally heal in time. When the Spirit's varied gifts of healing take place, there is a supernatural manifestation. It exceeds what we would consider a natural process. Again, being that there are a variety of healings, I believe this includes physical, emotional, psychological, mental, and spiritual.

To another the working of miracles.

This word "miracles" in the Greek means "power or force." It is the same Greek word used in Acts 1:8.

> *But you shall receive power when the Holy Spirit has come upon you; and you shall be witnesses to Me in Jerusalem, and in all Judea and Samaria, and to the end of the earth.*

This power, this force, is essential in sustaining an <u>impactful</u> witness. It's the power to change a life and save a soul. This same power is what Paul wrote about in his second letter to Timothy.

---

* *parenthetical mine*

For God has not given us a spirit of fear, but of power and of love and of a sound mind.

—2 Timothy 1:7

Having a form of godliness but denying its power. And from such people turn away!

—2 Timothy 3:5

I personally believe this power surrounds us every day of our lives, and if we're looking for it, we will see miracles happening all around us. At times, these miraculous events become clear demonstrations that God is working in our midst.

To another prophecy.

Prophecy simply means "inspired speaking, a foreteller." Let's let the Bible define this for us by using Revelation.

And I fell at his feet to worship him. But he said to me, "See that you do not do that! I am your fellow servant, and of your brethren who have the testimony of Jesus. Worship God! <u>For the testimony of Jesus is the spirit of prophecy.</u>"

—Revelation 19:10[*]

Whenever we share Christ, there is the spirit of prophecy. He is the same yesterday, today, and forever. His future

---

[*] *emphasis added*

promises are still being played out. His Word will come to pass fulfilling in time till the end of days. JESUS IS LORD!

To another discerning of spirits.

When you know the spirit of truth as your foundation, you will be able to recognize opposing spirits. This is the one gift that I wish for every believer. I once knew a woman who got a new job at a bank. For the first two weeks, they had her counting money in the basement all day long. By the end of the day, her hands were discolored from handling all the bills. Then, after two weeks, they slipped in a few counterfeit bills, and she recognized them simply by touch. The moral of the story is, if you know the truth, you will recognize when something is a lie.

I compare discernment to our taste buds on our tongues. You can discern if something is sweet or sour, salty or spicy. When you operate in the gift of discernment, you can spiritually taste or smell something fowl or tainted.

To another different kinds of tongues, to another the interpretation of tongues.

These two gifts are probably the most controversial, and I believe it's because they are not fully understood. Allow me to simplify, maybe oversimplify a common baseline.

1. "Various kinds of tongues" are in the plural. This could refer to international languages but also includes spiritual languages as Paul states in 1 Corinthians 13:

"Though I speak in the tongues <u>of men and of angels</u>." Here Paul refers to a heavenly language of angels.

2. I believe we speak in tongues before we learn our parents' language. Could we include tongues of babies? I think so, and moms usually have the interpretations. The baby cries in a certain way, and Mom says, "Oh, he's hungry," or she grumbles in a growl and Mom says, "She needs to be changed." Yeah, it's kinda like that.

3. I compare a spiritual language to crying or laughing. You can go to any country around the world and start to cry, and they will understand what you're saying. Or they see you belly laughing and will probably laugh along. They know what you're saying.

4. Music is also a spiritual language. It can convey deep emotions and carries an impact.

5. The first time tongues are mentioned in the Bible is at the Tower of Babel. When God wanted to divide mankind, He touched their tongue. It only makes sense to me that if God wanted to reunite mankind by His Spirit, He would again touch their tongue as He did at Pentecost.

6. These forms of tongues are meant to be used for public edification. So there will be times when someone speaks in a tongue in a public service. This, according to Scripture, demands an interpretation in order that things are done in order for the common good. I have seen this done well, and I have seen this done poorly. But we must never lose our primary focus of being led

by the Holy Spirit. There are occasions when the Holy Spirit wants to have direct input into our times together, and that can be clumsy. But I like to think that there are times when we need to not be in control. I embrace those awkward, divine interruptions . . . Jesus is Lord.

> *All these are empowered by one and the same Spirit, who apportions to each one individually as he wills.*[*]

You know, this whole realm of the Holy Spirit being in control really is a rub to organized religion. I'm sorry to say this, but it's true. When I was pastoring a large church, I often wondered who was really directing things. I know the Lord was there and was dominantly leading at times, but other times it was just murky.

I remember being a young pastor just starting out in ministry. I was in my office reading Scripture, and I came across the text when Jesus said, "I will build my church, and the gates of hell shall not prevail against it" (Matthew 16:18). But when I read it, the *I will build my church* came out much louder. It was as if He slapped my hand back in order to make sure I was clear of who was doing what. I believe He is still at work doing just that, but much of His building is being done outside the four walls.

Verses 12 through 26 really lay out how we are individually connected to one body and that each member is a significant

---

[*] *emphasis added*

33

part, even though they may not be a prominent part. It states that we should not disqualify ourselves or others because they are operating differently. This section concludes with "If one member suffers, all suffer together; if one member is honored, all rejoice together." There's that "us" thing again. Read this following section slowly, for yourself, and see if some of the groundwork we have laid still applies.

> *For as the body is one and has many members, but all the members of that one body, being many, are one body, so also is Christ. For by one Spirit we were all baptized into one body—whether Jews or Greeks, whether slaves or free—and have all been made to drink into one Spirit. For in fact the body is not one member but many.*

> *If the foot should say, "Because I am not a hand, I am not of the body," is it therefore not of the body? And if the ear should say, "Because I am not an eye, I am not of the body," is it therefore not of the body? If the whole body were an eye, where would be the hearing? If the whole were hearing, where would be the smelling? But now God has set the members, each one of them, in the body just as He pleased. And if they were all one member, where would the body be?*

> *But now indeed there are many members, yet one body. And the eye cannot say to the hand, "I have no need of you"; nor again the head to the feet, "I have*

no need of you." No, much rather, those members of the body which seem to be weaker are necessary. And those members of the body which we think to be less honorable, on these we bestow greater honor; and our unpresentable parts have greater modesty, but our presentable parts have no need. But God composed the body, having given greater honor to that part which lacks it, that there should be no schism in the body, but that the members should have the same care for one another. And if one member suffers, all the members suffer with it; or if one member is honored, all the members rejoice with it.

—1 Corinthians 12:12–26

Now you are the body of Christ, and members individually. And God <u>has appointed</u> these in the church: first apostles, second prophets, third teachers, after that miracles, then gifts of healings, helps, administrations, varieties of tongues. Are all apostles? Are all prophets? Are all teachers? Are all workers of miracles? Do all have gifts of healings? Do all speak with tongues? Do all interpret? But earnestly desire the best gifts. And yet I show you a more excellent way.

—1 Corinthians 12:27–31[*]

It's important we view this with the right lens. The word for "appointed" is the word "set" in the King James Version.

[*] *emphasis added*

That word in the Greek means "to place in the widest application literally or figurative in a passive or horizontal posture, make, ordain, purpose, put, set forth, settle, sink down." I don't believe the order is meant to be a vertical structure but one that is horizontally sequenced. Like one would set stones in a foundation, you would lay one next to the other but in sequence. Verses 29 to 30 open up the variety of the gifts distributed by the Holy Spirit as well as their selected delegations. But verse 31 presents an interesting twist.

But earnestly desire the best gifts.

DESIRING THE HIGHER GIFTS IN THEIR PUREST EXPRESSION

My goal is to do an overview of 1 Corinthians 12,13 & 14. We will see that Paul qualifies "best gifts" by their maximum input to building up the church. It appears that we can earnestly desire a gift, so we obviously still have a role in this partnership. No one is "possessed" by these gifts, but God invites us to comply and coordinate with His work. All three of these chapters are meant to be comprehensive and inclusive in order to discover how these gifts should operate.

And yet I show you a more excellent way.

This is his introduction to the thirteenth chapter, meaning the "more excellent way" is that the gifts are to be operated by, in, and through the love of God. This also verifies our need to keep the Holy Spirit in the center and core of these spiritual gifts. In my many years of full-time ministry, I have come to recognize something: I, personally, don't always have enough love in me at the time to do what I sense the Lord telling me to do. Not only love, but other attributes as well, like kindness, or mercy or forgiveness.

Please allow me to share an example, a real-life situation. Years ago, I was deeply hurt by another believer and no matter how many times I tried to forgive them, it didn't happen. I mean, I spoke it out, "I forgive them," but at the bottom of my heart was an unmovable boulder. One early morning in prayer, I again felt this stone and literally cried to God for it to be removed. And all of a sudden, I heard something that really stunned me. What I heard was, "You know, Jesus didn't forgive those who crucified Him at the cross." WHAT? It shook me to my core. I have preached many times the seven cries of the cross, and I know what happened there. But then I heard this: He said, "FATHER, forgive them, for they know not what they do." So the point was that Jesus asked the Father and did not just muster up forgiveness in himself. I knew exactly what I had to do, so I prayed, "Father, forgive them," and that's as far as I got. There was such a rush of grace that flowed through my soul. That rock flushed out of me and left in its wake a cleansing deliverance that is still liberating and restoring my soul. By asking the Father, I tapped into His unlimited supply of grace, love, mercy, kindness, and forgiveness. You see, there are times when we do not possess the essential power to do the work of God and must turn to His power, His Spirit to actually accomplish His work, His way.

While the tears of cleansing washed through me, I was reminded of the Lord's Prayer where it says, "Forgive us our trespasses as we forgive those who trespass against us." I looked up the word "as"—I know, I'm a word nerd. This word means "while, when, as" so "as" we're talking, "while" we're talking and "when" we're talking is the same thing. So let me explain what happened. As I forgave, when I forgave, and while I forgave, I was forgiven. "Forgive us while we're forgiving," "forgive us when we forgive." It all happens simultaneously. While we forgive, we are forgiven. While that rush of mercy and grace flowed through me, it cleaned me too. Hallelujah!!! Amen!

1 Corinthians 13

We need to take this chapter as a continuation of chapter 12. Paul here goes back over the gifts he just mentioned and qualifies them. These gifts must be utilized by the same spirit and that spirit is love. If you remember earlier, I mentioned how I've seen gifts used in the wrong spirit. I've seen people shamed, humiliated, and actually cursed by a supposed gift of prophecy. A wrong spirit disqualifies the gift.

> *Though I speak with the tongues of men and of angels, but have not love, I have become sounding brass or a clanging cymbal. And though I have the gift of prophecy, and understand all mysteries and all knowledge, and though I have all faith, so that I could remove*

mountains, but have not love, I am nothing. And though I bestow all my goods to feed the poor, and though I give my body to be burned, but have not love, it profits me nothing.

—1 Corinthians 13:1–3

We see this also abused by today's church in general. Not only the church, but the world as well. "Oh, we should just love everyone no matter who or what they are." The thing I appreciate about Paul's writing here is that he doesn't leave us to describe our own definition of love, but actually develops love's qualities and attributes.

Love suffers long and is kind; love does not envy; love does not parade itself, is not puffed up; does not behave rudely, does not seek its own, is not provoked, thinks no evil; does not rejoice in iniquity, but rejoices in the truth; bears all things, believes all things, hopes all things, endures all things. Love never fails.

—1 Corinthians 13:4–8

This section of Scripture gives us a wonderful filter we can use before operating in a gift. If we go back to understanding gifts as appliances, even in our chores around the house, there is a base of love. Now, that doesn't mean we're always happy about it. But the underlying aspect of love should always be there.

There was a time when I had a word of knowledge about something hidden in an individual. I had the opportunity to publicly expose them but didn't. I put myself in their shoes and prayed about them first. I checked my own heart whether I had love in my heart for them. It changed everything. We were able to deal with this privately and before the Lord. The end result was deliverance and redemption. So, verses 4 through 8 are something you should read before you desire to operate in any gifts. Get your heart tuned into the Holy Spirit, the right spirit. Verse 6 gives another insight into love.

> <u>Does not rejoice</u> in <u>iniquity</u>, but rejoices in the truth.*

If you hold this next to Hebrews 12:4–14, it gives further insight into love.

> You have not yet resisted to bloodshed, striving against sin. And you have forgotten the exhortation which speaks to you as to sons: "My son, do not despise the chastening of the Lord, nor be discouraged when you are rebuked by Him; for whom the Lord loves He chastens, and scourges every son whom He receives."
>
> If you endure chastening, God deals with you as with sons; for what son is there whom a father does not chasten? But if you are without chastening, of which all have become partakers, then you are illegitimate and not sons. Furthermore, we have had human

---

* emphasis added

41

fathers who corrected us, and we paid them respect. Shall we not much more readily be in subjection to the Father of spirits and live? For they indeed for a few days chastened us as seemed best to them, but He for our profit, that we may be partakers of His holiness. Now no chastening seems to be joyful for the present, but painful; nevertheless, afterward it yields the peaceable fruit of righteousness to those who have been trained by it.

Therefore strengthen the hands which hang down, and the feeble knees, and make straight paths for your feet, so that what is lame may not be dislocated, but rather be healed. Pursue peace with all people, and holiness, without which no one will see the Lord.

Love disciplines for our good. Our good is to grow into holiness, and without holiness no one will see the Lord. Let's continue in chapter 13.

But whether there are prophecies, they will fail; whether there are tongues, they will cease; whether there is knowledge, it will vanish away. For we know in part and we prophesy in part. But when that which is perfect has come, then that which is in part will be done away.

When I was a child, I spoke as a child, I understood as a child, I thought as a child; but when I became a man, I put away childish things. For now we see in a mirror,

*dimly, but then face to face. Now I know in part, but
then I shall know just as I also am known.*

—*1 Corinthians 13:8–12*

This portion is unfortunately used to quench the gifts of
the Spirit. Some say that the gifts were only for the apostolic
age or dispensation. It's regrettable to me that this disquali-
fication, this rejection, has contributed to much of the loss of
the Church's power. They believe that now that we have the
Bible, the whole counsel of God, we no longer need these gifts.
I agree that the Bible is the whole counsel of God . . . so why
are they taking out the gifts from the whole counsel of God?
THEY'RE IN THE BIBLE!

Another thing I ask when I'm discussing this with someone
is, "Has the power of sin changed or diminished?" Obviously, it
hasn't. Then why would the solution and cure be diminished?

It is clear to me that when Paul is stating, "But when that
which is perfect has come, then that which is in part will be
done away," he is speaking of the return of Christ and His
kingdom. Only then will we no longer be needing these gifts.
Read verses 11 through 12.

> *When I was a child, I spoke as a child, I understood as
> a child, I thought as a child; but when I became a man,
> I put away childish things. For now we see in a mirror,
> dimly, but then <u>face to face</u>. Now I know in part, but
> then I shall know just as I also am known.*[*]

---

[*] *emphasis added*

I remember once watching the Discovery Channel, and they were showing a Lion's pride in the wild. At one point, the camera focused on the young cubs stalking and pouncing on each other. The Lord spoke to me and compared them to His Church. When the spiritual gifts are a "new thing" to us, we play with them. We turn them on each other and think we are really doing well. But then the Lord said that when the Church becomes mature in these gifts, they will use them as tools, even weapons against the powers of darkness and in delivering souls from captivity. As children, we play, but as adults, we work. Unfortunately, many are still playing church and not really willing to use their gifts in the real world.

A quote by Charles Kingsley can apply to this issue: "We worship at our work, we work at our play, and we play at our worship." I'd like you to try and comprehend your sphere of influence. Your neighborhood, your school, your shopping circuit—any and all interactive venues. Because that is your realm to operate the gifts of the Holy Spirit. If you are exclusively operating only within the walls of the church, it can contribute to developing a double mindedness. The reason being, we separate our spiritual life at church from our "normal" lives, and rarely are we willing to "be spiritual" in the real world.

> And now abide faith, hope, love, these three; but the greatest of these is love.
>
> —1 Corinthians 13:13

Now let's look into the fourteenth chapter.

> *Pursue love, and desire spiritual gifts, but especially that you may prophesy. For he who speaks in a tongue does not speak to men but to God, for no one understands him; however, <u>in the spirit he speaks mysteries</u>.*
>
> *—1 Corinthians 14:1-2*[*]

There is something expressed in the above two verses that is radical in its distinction, not only because they distinguish between an understandable gift of prophesy and the less understandable gift of tongues but also because this expression of tongues is intrinsically different from the tongues mentioned earlier in chapter 12. Paul begins verse 1 by establishing a sequence or an organized priority. First, pursue love. Again, the greatest of these is love! He emphasizes that love should be our first pursuit.

> *By this we know love, because He laid down His life for us. And we also ought to lay down our lives for the brethren. But whoever has this world's goods, and sees his brother in need, and shuts up his heart from him, how does the love of God abide in him? My little children, let us not love in word or in tongue, but in deed and in truth.*
>
> *—1 John 3:16–18*

---

[*] *emphasis added*

Here we have again the challenge to embrace our plural us-ness identity by loving the brethren more than our own lives: "<u>Pursue love</u>, and <u>earnestly desire</u> the spiritual gifts."

Both are verbs; pursue means "to make to run or flee, put to flight, drive away, to run swiftly in order to catch a person or thing, to run after, to seek after eagerly, earnestly endeavor to acquire" (Strongs). Desire means "to burn with zeal, to be heated or to boil with envy, in a good sense, to be zealous in the pursuit of good, to desire earnestly, pursue, to desire one earnestly, to strive after, busy one's self about him, to exert one's self for one (that he may not be torn from me), to be the object of the zeal of others, to be zealously sought after (Strongs).

Let's approach this from the reverse. Considering the definitions of pursuit and desire, what do you already chase after or long for? What drives you with zeal or envy? If you can answer these questions, you'll understand what motivates you. One major issue today is the many distractions. The key question is not about whether we can pursue or desire, but if we can focus these on God. You can't fill an already full cup. To follow this scriptural direction, some personal reflection and clearing out the house may be needed. We deceive ourselves if we say, "God you are number one, but then spend all our time and resource actually pursuing numbers two, three, four, and five. If you want to see what people are driven by, you can look two places: their calendar and their checkbook. Where we spend our time and our resources can reveal what we pursue and desire.

Let's look again at the opening verses of 1 Corinthians 14.

Pursue love, and desire spiritual gifts, but especially that you may prophesy. For he who speaks in a tongue does not speak to men but to God, for no one understands him; however, in the spirit he speaks mysteries.

—1 Corinthians 14:1–2

Paul here seems to put at odds what appear to be two competing gifts. But if you remember our previous reading of the gifts in chapter 12, he refers to various gifts of "tongues" in the plural, here he speaks in the singular "tongue." I believe the distinction here is not to disqualify this gift of a tongue, but to recognize that he is stating a separation in the focus of this gift. Tongues and interpretation, along with prophecy, has a focus on the Church. But there is a tongue that is focused toward God. This is intended for personal prayer in strengthening our own spirit with encouragement as well as perfectly praying things beyond our own understanding.

Likewise the Spirit also helps in our weaknesses. For we do not know what we should pray for as we ought, but the Spirit Himself makes intercession for us with <u>groanings which cannot be uttered</u>. Now He who searches the hearts knows what the mind of the Spirit is, because <u>He makes intercession for the saints</u> according to the will of God.

And we know that all things work together for good to those who love God, to those who are the called according to His purpose. For whom He foreknew, He also predestined to be conformed to the image of His Son, that He might be the firstborn among many brethren. Moreover whom He predestined, these He also called; whom He called, these He also justified; and whom He justified, these He also glorified.

—Romans 8:26–30*

For this reason I bow my knees to the Father [a]of our Lord Jesus Christ, from whom the whole family in heaven and earth is named, that He would grant you, according to the riches of His glory, to be <u>strengthened with might through His Spirit in the inner man</u>, that Christ may dwell in your hearts through faith; that you, being rooted and grounded in love, may be able to comprehend with all the saints what is the width and length and depth and height—to know the love of Christ <u>which passes knowledge</u>; that you may <u>be filled with all the fullness of God</u>.

—Ephesians 3:14–19*

It is vitally important for us to understand this distinction especially considering our opening premise of appliances. The gifts focus on the Church; therefore, they are appliance gifts.

---

* *emphasis added*

But this gift is unique in that it is exclusively for the believer's edification and strengthening. Friends, this is not an appliance gift, but rather this is the diamond ring, this is the freshwater pearls. This is the gift God gives you FOR YOU! This gift is part of your inner circle. As you contemplate this distinction in focus, I believe the remainder of this chapter will come into further clarity.

Let's look at a big chunk of this chapter.

> *Pursue love, and desire spiritual gifts, but especially that you may prophesy. For he who speaks in a tongue does not speak to men but to God, for no one understands him; however, in the spirit he speaks mysteries. But he who prophesies speaks edification and exhortation and comfort to men. He who speaks in a tongue edifies himself, but he who prophesies edifies the church. I wish you all spoke with tongues, but even more that you prophesied; for he who prophesies is greater than he who speaks with tongues, unless indeed he interprets, that the church may receive edification.*
>
> *But now, brethren, if I come to you speaking with tongues, what shall I profit you unless I speak to you either by revelation, by knowledge, by prophesying, or by teaching? Even things without life, whether flute or harp, when they make a sound, unless they make a distinction in the sounds, how will it be known what is piped or played? For if the trumpet makes an*

uncertain sound, who will prepare for battle? So likewise you, unless you utter by the tongue words easy to understand, how will it be known what is spoken? For you will be speaking into the air. There are, it may be, so many kinds of languages in the world, and none of them is without significance. Therefore, if I do not know the meaning of the language, I shall be a foreigner to him who speaks, and he who speaks will be a foreigner to me. Even so you, since you are zealous for spiritual gifts, let it be for the edification of the church that you seek to excel.

Therefore let him who speaks in a tongue pray that he may interpret. For if I pray in a tongue, my spirit prays, but my understanding is unfruitful. What is the conclusion then? I will pray with the spirit, and I will also pray with the understanding. I will sing with the spirit, and I will also sing with the understanding. Otherwise, if you bless with the spirit, how will he who occupies the place of the uninformed say "Amen" at your giving of thanks, since he does not understand what you say? For you indeed give thanks well, but the other is not edified.

I thank my God I speak with tongues more than you all; yet in the church I would rather speak five words with my understanding, that I may teach others also, than ten thousand words in a tongue.

—1 Corinthians 14:1–19

I know that was a boat load, but hopefully you can see the bigger picture here. Allow me to state some of the key takeaways:

- Paul distinguishes between two primary gifts: one focused toward God and the other toward the Church.

- He indicates that both gifts contribute to edification and strength: one for personal development and the other for the community or congregation.

- Consider the items in your home. You can likely distinguish those meant for personal use from the appliances.

- Earlier, I used music as an example of tongues, and Paul makes a similar comparison.

- Paul emphasizes gifts that edify and strengthen the Church, such as prophecy, within the church community. This does not eliminate the personal gift of speaking in tongues but clarifies where it should be applied—unless there is an interpretation.

- Verse 15 clearly embraces both gifts: *What is the conclusion then? I will pray with the spirit, and I will also pray with the understanding. I will sing with the spirit, and I will also sing with the understanding.* Here bridging the validity of both.

- Also verses 17 and 18 affirm the benefits of this spiritual prayer and thanksgiving. *For you indeed give thanks well, but the other is not edified. I thank my God I speak with tongues more than you all.*

Brethren, do not be children in understanding; however, in malice be babes, but in understanding be mature. In the law it is written:

"With men of other tongues and other lips I will speak to this people; and yet, for all that, they will not hear Me," says the Lord.

Therefore tongues are for a sign, not to those who believe but to unbelievers; but prophesying is not for unbelievers but for those who believe. Therefore if the whole church comes together in one place, and all speak with tongues, and there come in those who are uninformed or unbelievers, will they not say that you are out of your mind? But if all prophesy, and an unbeliever or an uninformed person comes in, he is convinced by all, he is convicted by all. And thus the secrets of his heart are revealed; and so, falling down on his face, he will worship God and report that God is truly among you.

—*1 Corinthians 14:20-25*

This portion begins to deal with the inclusion of unbelievers. Unbelievers or outsiders are to be a consideration in the way we conduct our times together. There has been much emphasis on this aspect over the past thirty years. The "seeker sensitive" model was widely embraced, and it did facilitate church growth in numbers. But one has to ask if this approach has actually strengthened the Church. The church I started began with seventeen people and grew significantly. I witnessed firsthand how this growth led to changes in operations and focus. We had new visitors every Sunday, but we lost intimacy and power. Although I maintained my personal convictions, increased staff and delegated authority reduced my influence. By the time I retired, the leadership's focus had shifted to attendance and finances. Or, as I like to say, "nickels and noses." In fact, as we look to the following text in this chapter, we should be deeply challenged and honestly reassess the format we currently use in our gatherings.

> How is it then, brethren? Whenever you come together, each of you has a psalm, has a teaching, has a tongue, has a revelation, has an interpretation. Let all things be done for edification. If anyone speaks in a tongue, let there be two or at the most three, each in turn, and let one interpret. But if there is no interpreter, let him keep silent in church, and let him speak to himself and to God. Let two or three prophets speak, and let the others judge. But if anything is revealed to another who sits by, let the first keep silent. For you can all prophesy one by one, that all may learn and all may be encouraged. And the spirits of the prophets are subject to the prophets. For God is not the author of confusion but of peace, as in all the churches of the saints.
>
> —1 Corinthians 14:26–33

Verse 26 gives us a startling construct that seems to indicate each one attending should come with something to contribute to the gathering—a hymn, a lesson, a revelation, a tongue or interpretation. Just imagine what this format would look like in real time. Allow me to make some presumed inferences here.

1. It would have to be a smaller group.
2. Everyone would have to be likeminded and humbly submitted to the Holy Spirit.
3. A common purpose or goal would be to build up and strengthen the assembly by each edifying one another.
4. While embracing those the Lord would add to our meetings.

> If anyone speaks in a tongue, let there be two or at the most three, each in turn, and let one interpret.
>
> —1 Corinthians 14:27

OK, verse 27 clearly states that tongues could be a contributing part to our service time. In fact, there should be two or three expressions as long as someone interprets. There goes the neighborhood. Can you imagine this in your church? What do you think would be the result? First, in many churches it would not be allowed. So why not?

> But if there is no interpreter, let him keep silent in church, and let him <u>speak to himself and to God</u>.
>
> —1 Corinthians 14:28[*]

---

[*] *emphasis added*

This verse tells us to be vigilant and discerning as to the presence of someone with the gift of interpretation. Believe me, this is easier said than done. But in the case that an interpreter is not available, we are to speak to God silently. In context, I believe this is saying pray in the Spirit silently. Here again is the mention of the personal edification of a tongue prayer language.

> *Let two or three prophets speak, and let the others judge. But if anything is revealed to another who sits by, let the first keep silent. For you can all prophesy one by one, that all may learn and all may be encouraged. And the spirits of the prophets are subject to the prophets. For God is not the author of confusion but of peace, as in all the churches of the saints.*
>
> *—1 Corinthians 14:29–33*

Here we go! In everything we read to this point, Paul declares a preference to prophecy over tongues. And many use this emphasis to diminish and even disqualify the gift of tongues. Well, then, I'm sure there must be several who prophecy within their meetings, right? Two or three? Verse 31 says we can ALL prophesy one by one. Again, can you imagine? What Paul is attempting to do is establish a balance between spiritual gifts being allowed to operate and function, but in order. Why are so many afraid to allow this direct influence of the Holy Spirit? Is there a fear of losing control?

> *And the spirits of the prophets are subject to the prophets.*
>
> —*1 Corinthians 14:32*

This verse is key to understanding the operation of the gifts. The spirit is subject or in submission to the prophets. I have experienced meetings where they are out of control. Their excuse is, "The Holy Spirit told me to do it." My first response is, "Do not blame that on the Holy Spirit because there was nothing holy in it." Again, the Holy Spirit does not possess you, but rather partners with you. This blend only happens when we take the time to use our personal prayer language and strengthen our relationship in and with the Holy Spirit. Paul is saying that the Holy Spirit will yield to the prophet. And that is not quenching the Holy Spirit but partnering with Him.

> *For God is not the author of confusion but of peace, as in all the churches of the saints.*
>
> *Let your women keep silent in the churches, for they are not permitted to speak; but they are to be submissive, as the law also says. And if they want to learn something, let them ask their own husbands at home; for it is shameful for women to speak in church.*
>
> *Or did the word of God come originally from you? Or was it you only that it reached? If anyone thinks himself to be a prophet or spiritual, let him acknowledge that the things which I write to you are the*

commandments of the Lord. But if anyone is ignorant,
let him be ignorant.

—1 Corinthians 14:33–38

Verses 33 through 38 are dealing with an issue that is outside the focus of this book. We are focused on the gifts of the Holy Spirit, but here Paul deals with other aspects of church order. But I would like to look at this as it relates to gifts.

Be diligent to present yourself approved to God, a
worker who does not need to be ashamed, <u>rightly di-</u>
<u>viding the word of truth</u>.

—2 Timothy 2:15*

Let's look at other scriptures where women take part in the operating the gifts of the Spirit. When Peter stood up at the Day of Pentecost and spoke from the Prophet Joel.

But this is what was spoken by the prophet Joel:
And it shall come to pass in the last days, says God,
That I will pour out of My Spirit on all flesh;
Your sons and your <u>daughters shall prophesy,</u>
Your young men shall see visions,
Your old men shall dream dreams.
And on My menservants and on <u>My maidservants</u>
<u>I will pour out My Spirit in those days;</u>
<u>And they shall prophesy</u>.

—Acts 2:16–18*

---

* *emphasis added*

But before faith came, we were kept under guard by the law, kept for the faith which would afterward be revealed. Therefore the law was our tutor to bring us to Christ, that we might be justified by faith. But after faith has come, we are no longer under a tutor. For you are all sons of God through faith in Christ Jesus. For as many of you as were baptized into Christ have put on Christ. There is neither Jew nor Greek, there is neither slave nor free, there is neither male nor female; for you are all one in Christ Jesus. And if you are Christ's, then you are Abraham's seed, and heirs according to the promise.

—Galatians 3:23-29*

Several women in the Bible are recognized as prophetesses, playing significant roles in their communities and conveying divine messages. Here are a few notable examples:

- **Miriam:** The sister of Moses and Aaron; she is called a prophetess and led the women of Israel in song and dance after crossing the Red Sea (Exodus 15:20–21).

- **Deborah:** A judge and prophetess, she provided guidance to Israel and played a key role in leading them to victory in battle (Judges 4:4–5).

- **Huldah:** Her prophecy was sought by King Josiah when the Book of the Law was discovered, influencing major religious reforms (2 Kings 22:14–20).

- **Anna**: A prophetess in the New Testament, she recognized Jesus as the Messiah and spoke about Him to those awaiting redemption (Luke 2:36–38).

- **Philip's daughters**: The four daughters of Philip the Evangelist are mentioned as prophetesses in the New Testament (Acts 21:8–9).

These women did exemplify spiritual gifts and the ability to inspire change.

> *Therefore, brethren, desire earnestly to prophesy, and <u>do not forbid to speak with tongues</u>. Let all things be done decently and in order.*
>
> *—1 Corinthians 14:39-40**

Once again, Paul encourages the desire to prophesy as he has established the priority of strengthening the Church. But lest this emphasis should be misinterpreted, he is sure to underscore that this does not disqualify the gift of tongues and that tongues should not be forbidden.

Now, before we conclude our time together, I would like to take a step back from all the gifts we've spoken about and look to an underlying essential attribute that will determine the access and release of these gifts in your life.

JESUS IS LORD!

> *Thus says the LORD:*
> *"Heaven is My throne,*

---

* *emphasis added*

And earth is My footstool.
Where is the house that you will build Me?
And where is the place of My rest?
For all those things My hand has made,
And all those things exist,"
Says the Lord.
"But on this one will I look:
On him who is poor and of a contrite spirit,
And who trembles at My word."

—Isaiah 66:1–2

"Jesus is Lord" is not merely a declaration or statement; it is a heart trembling, awe-inspired, reality check that Jesus is above all principalities and powers. And at the name of Jesus, every knee will bow and every **tongue** confess that Jesus Christ is Lord to the Glory of God the Father. Only by walking in a humble position can we ever hope to be used by the Holy Spirit to manifest His powerful gifts.

Therefore if there is any consolation in Christ, if any comfort of love, if any fellowship of the Spirit, if any affection and mercy, fulfill my joy by being like-minded, having the same love, being of one accord, of one mind. Let nothing be done through selfish ambition or conceit, but in lowliness of mind let each esteem others better than himself. Let each of you look out not only for his own interests, but also for the interests of others.

Let this mind be in you which was also in Christ Jesus, who, being in the form of God, did not consider it robbery to be equal with God, but made Himself of no reputation, taking the form of a bondservant, and coming in the likeness of men. And being found in appearance as a man, He humbled Himself and became obedient to the point of death, even the death of the cross. Therefore God also has highly exalted Him and given Him the name which is above every name, that at the name of Jesus every knee should bow, of those in heaven, and of those on earth, and of those under the earth, and that every tongue should confess that Jesus Christ is Lord, to the glory of God the Father Father.

—Philippians 2:1-11[*]

The above scripture actually builds the platform by which we can function as fellow members of the Body of Christ. This is key and required to truly be able to speak "Jesus is Lord." This mindset is radically different than how we are taught by the world to function. "Look out for number one" seems to be the mantra. You can make a smooth transition from that platform by simply making Jesus number one.

He has told you, O man, what is good;
and what does the LORD require of you
but to do justice, and to love kindness,

---

[*] *emphasis added*

and to <u>walk humbly with your God</u>?

—Micah 6:8*

If you have a clear image of who it is we worship, if you have comprehended the vast domain in which our God reigns, if you see that our God is a sovereign God who rules and over-rules, It's pretty easy to walk humbly with Him. So don't try to just humble yourself—try to get a fuller picture of who it is that saves you and delivers you. The all-authority victor of the universe.

> *By humility and the fear of the Lord are riches and honor and life.*
>
>
>
> *—Proverbs 22:4*
>
>

This scripture works in tandem with Hebrews 11:6:

> *But without faith it is impossible to please Him, for he who comes to God must believe that He is, and that He is a rewarder of those who diligently seek Him.*

Could this reward in part allow us to be used by the Holy Spirit to partner with His work on the earth?

> *But <u>He gives more grace</u>. Therefore He says: "God resists the proud, <u>but gives grace to the humble</u>." Therefore submit to God. Resist the devil and he will flee from you. Draw near to God and He will draw near to you. Cleanse your hands, you sinners; and purify*

your hearts, you double-minded. Lament and mourn and weep! Let your laughter be turned to mourning and your joy to gloom. Humble yourselves in the sight of the Lord, and He will lift you up.

—James 4:6–10[*]

Remember earlier we read that gifts are the extension of grace. *Charis* to *Charisma*. So God gives more grace to the humble—more potential for gifts to operate.

Likewise you younger people, submit yourselves to your elders. Yes, all of you be submissive to one another, and be clothed with humility, for "God resists the proud, but gives grace to the humble." Therefore humble yourselves under the mighty hand of God, that He may exalt you in due time, casting all your care upon Him, for He cares for you.

—1 Peter 5:5–7

So, Jesus is Lord! As we continue in a sincere walk with Him, we can maintain a humble position next to Him. Also remember that love is the spirit behind the gifts. When you really love, you're willing to surrender pride, prestige, or position and humbly show others they are more important.

I pray that as you have followed along in this study, you have come to appreciate this spiritual realm of the Gifts of the Spirit. My hope is that the gifts were de-mystified and

---

[*] *emphasis added*

made clearer in their operation, priority, and essential value. We are called throughout Scripture to walk in the Spirit and walk in love. I hope now you will not only embrace this realm as obtainable, but also understand the amount of riches God has extended to us as members of the Body of Christ.

JESUS IS LORD!

FINAL THOUGHTS

I f you are wondering how you can begin, as Paul wrote: "Pursue love, and desire spiritual gifts" (1 Corinthians 14:1). "Pursue" and "desire" start with you. But how do we get to that place? How do we begin this quest? Please allow me to make some personal suggestions from my own experience as well as helping others break through into this realm of the Spirits Gifts.

1. **Develop your prayer muscle.**

   We all understand how exercising muscle groups can strengthen those parts of the body. Same can be said for our spiritual development. How strong is your prayer muscle? I encourage you to take on this challenge. Commit time to consecrated prayer. This is not the blessing over the food or God help me through today. Set apart a time and space of isolation, where you can be alone with God . . . and pray! Prayer is the first step to becoming more familiar with the Holy Spirit and sense His presence.

2. **Seek to develop a spiritual prayer language.**

   This is the diamond we referred to in 1 Corinthians 14:2. For he who speaks in a tongue does not speak to men but to God, for no one understands him; however, in the spirit he speaks mysteries. This simply allows your spirit to groan. Again, I compared this to laughing or crying. It's expressing deep longings or broken heartedness. Don't listen to what you are saying because you're not talking to you, you are talking to the God who made you. God looks on the heart and I imagine He listens to it as well. Keep it simple and pure. Don't force it or fake it, just pray beyond words.

3. **Express your desire for spiritual gifts**

   Open yourself up to the idea that God can work through you in supernatural ways. It sounds scary, but in reality it all comes from the Holy Spirit, whom I believe you can fully trust. And like the lion cubs from the Discovery channel I referred to earlier, when you are with fellow believers ask God to use you. This is not meant to bring additional pressure to perform, this is an opportunity to grow.

4. **Continue to grow in grace.**

Remember that grace = *charis* and gift = *charisma*. As you grow in His grace for you, the gifts are in there also. You can grow into a fuller expression of His love and grace, and as you do, those expressions will take on a fuller manifestation of all He has to offer: healing, wisdom, knowledge, miracles. All these are part of His work and ministry, and He allows us to become partners in His kingdom. What a great Joy.

There are three levels of appliances: residential, commercial, and industrial. If God gives you a gift, start using it in your home. For many, this can be difficult because we think the gifts should only be used in a church setting. I believe it should start in the home! That is where our faith walk endures. If you start with a residential appliance and God increases the strength of your gift, it can grow into a commercial grade. And who knows, maybe even industrial. But that should not be your concern; begin right where you are and allow His grace and gifts to flow!

Wishing you the "blest"!

DEEP GLIMPSES SERIES

Having served in full-time ministry for over thirty-three years, I have delivered countless sermons and teachings. While many of these messages blur together, a select few stand out as profound revelations—insights that have left an indelible mark on my soul and fundamentally changed my life.

These messages emerged from personal transformative experiences and comprise the books featured here in the Deep Glimpses series.

Remembering Communion
Jesus instructed, "Do this in remembrance of me." As you approach communion, what do you remember? I identified a direct parallel between marriage and communion, noting that the elements we remember about marriage correspond directly to our relationship with Christ and one another. Furthermore, I believe that the Lord's Table should involve more interaction among believers, making the presented pattern inclusive and participative.

The Appliance Gifts
God bestows grace upon each of us, connecting us through gifts that serve the church by strengthening, encouraging,

and serving one another. These gifts function much like household appliances, contributing to a healthy and whole spiritual habitation.

The Author of Authority

In addition to being a pastor, I also led worship, fostering a dynamic culture within our worship experiences. However, there came a time when I questioned the direction and purpose of our focus in worship. Worship is far more than mere performance; it is a venue for exchange, impartation, and endowment. Understanding this can profoundly enhance the power in our lives.

Being Effective Between a Rock and a Hard Place

I often felt overwhelmed with ministry tasks such as counseling, leadership meetings, and sermon preparation, while balancing my marriage and family. In desperation, I cried out to the Lord, "I feel like I'm between a rock and a hard place. His response was, "That's where you should be," and He showed me biblical positions to help equip me in making the most of those times.

Lord willing, there will be other books in this series, but for now my prayer is that you will be strengthened and encouraged with these insights and brought into a clearer understanding of your walk with the living God.